Coloring book for adults and kids amazing cactus flower image for design

This coloring book is

belongs to

....

....

....

CACTI TO CACTI YO

Cactus

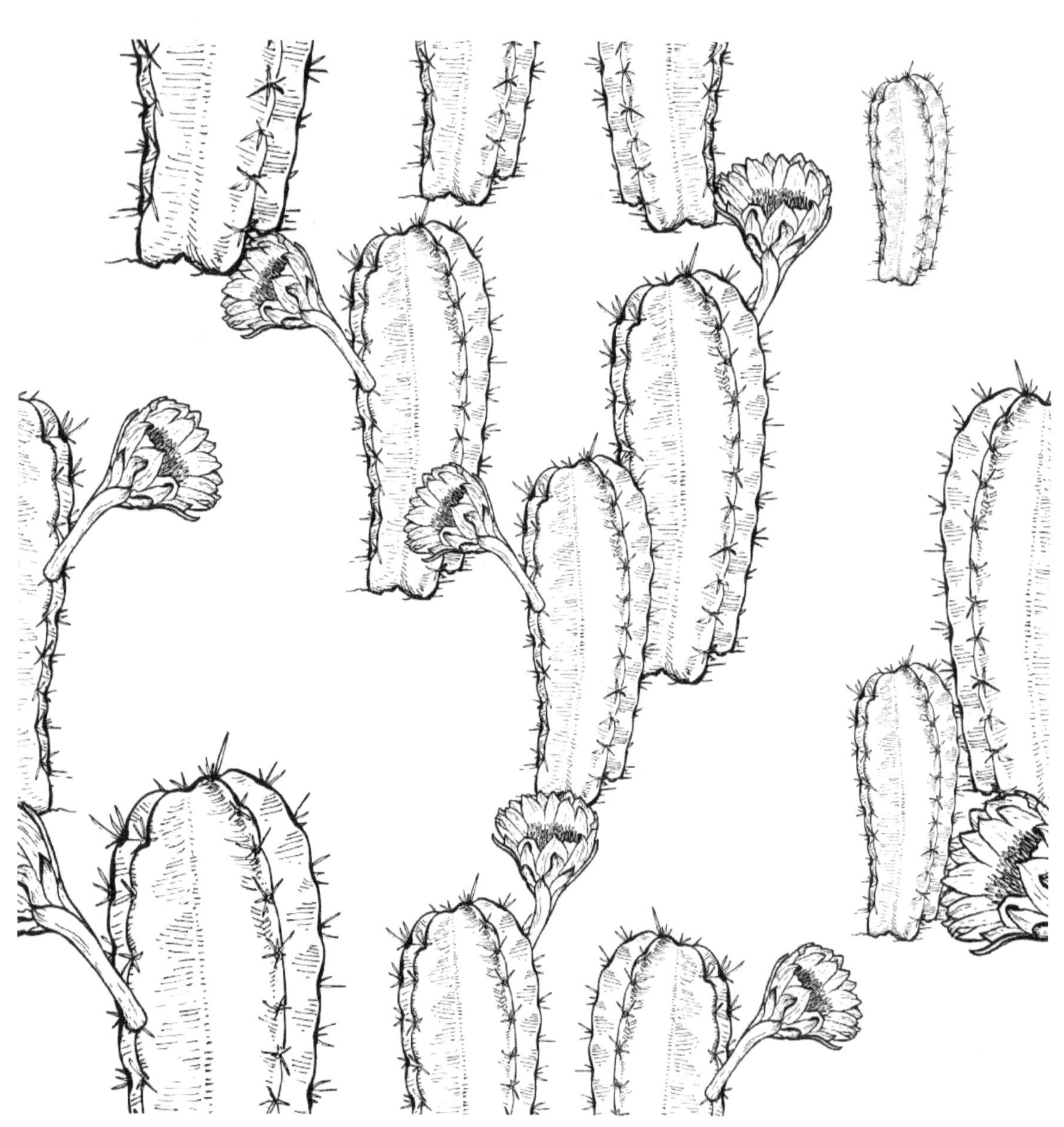

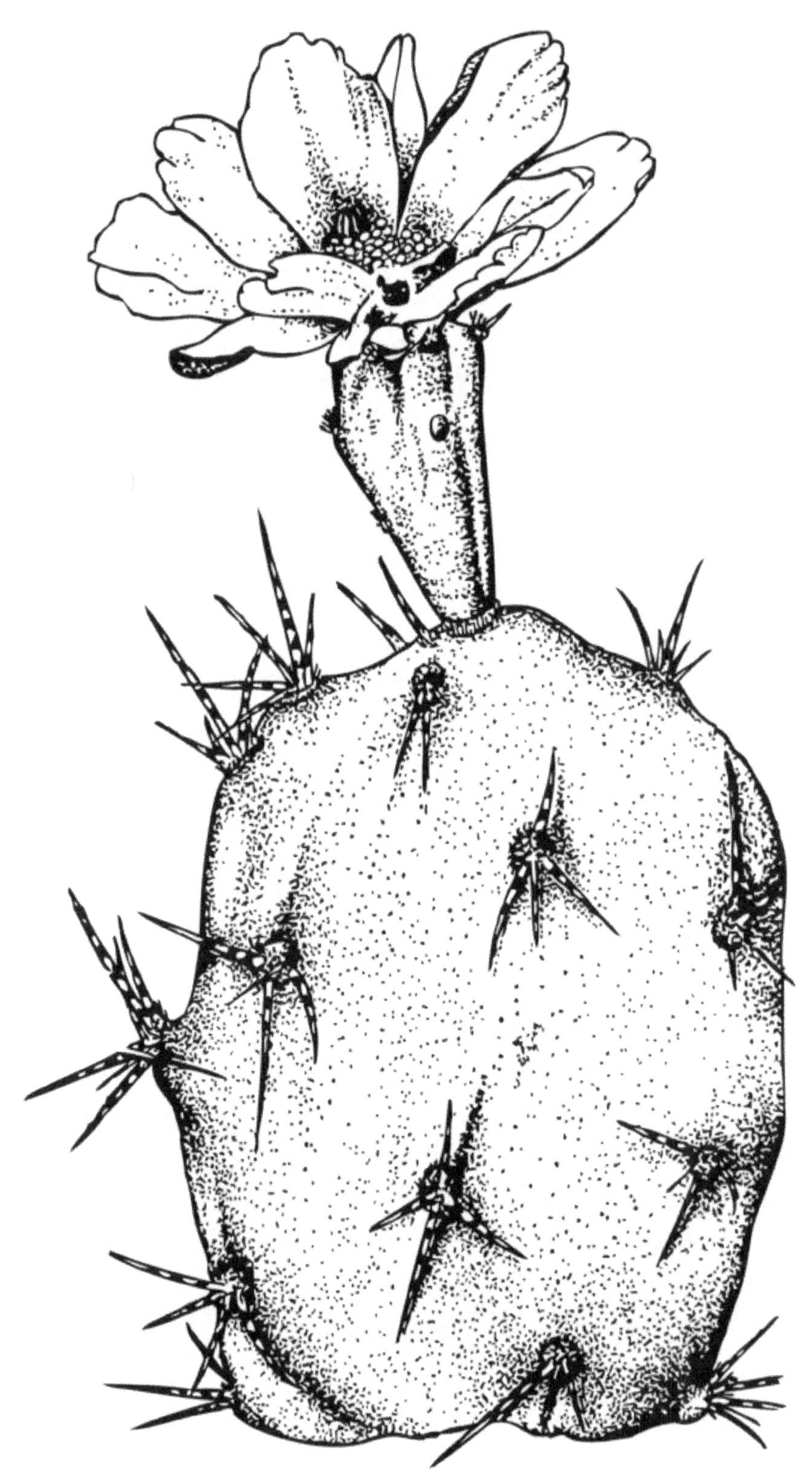

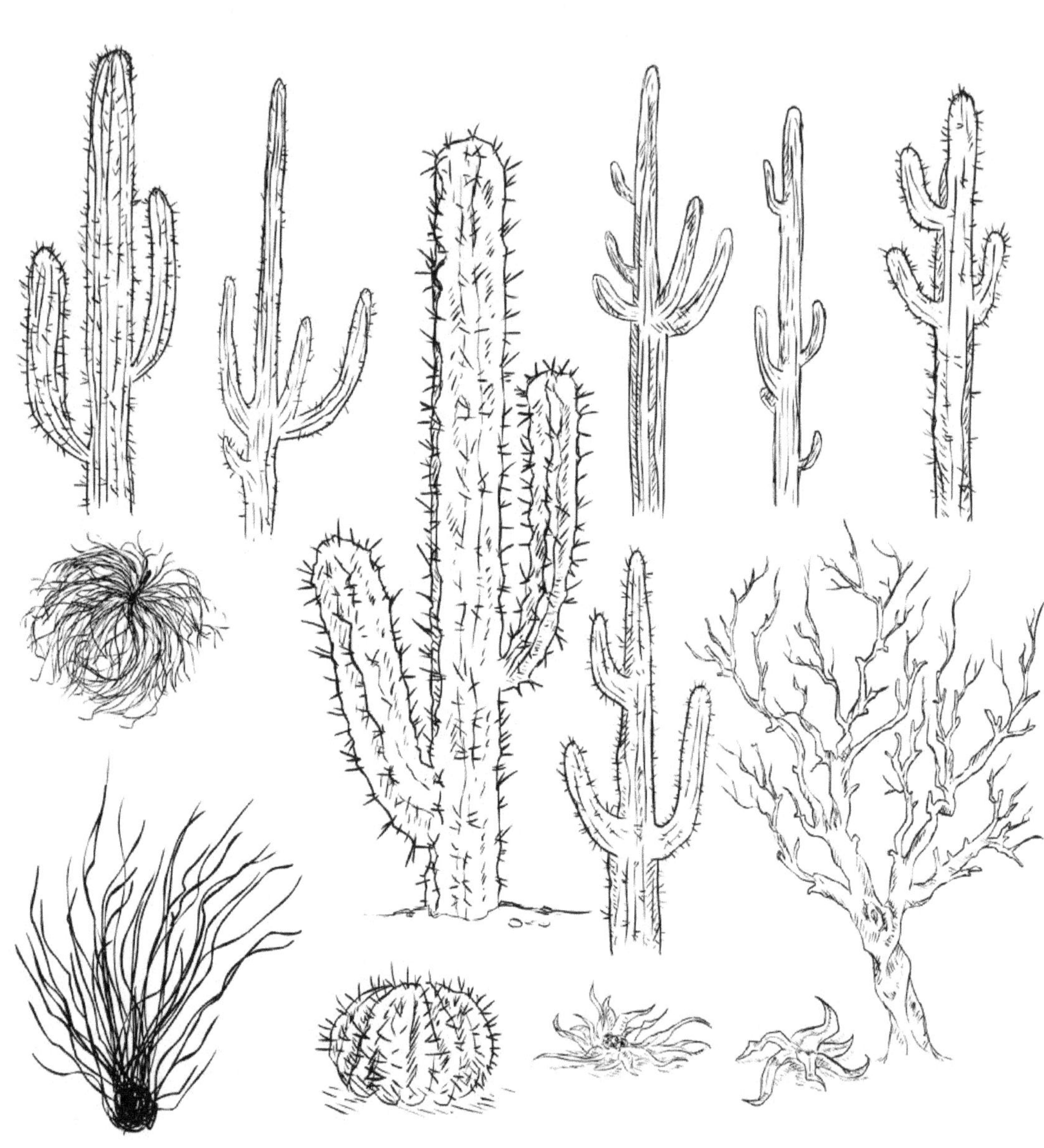

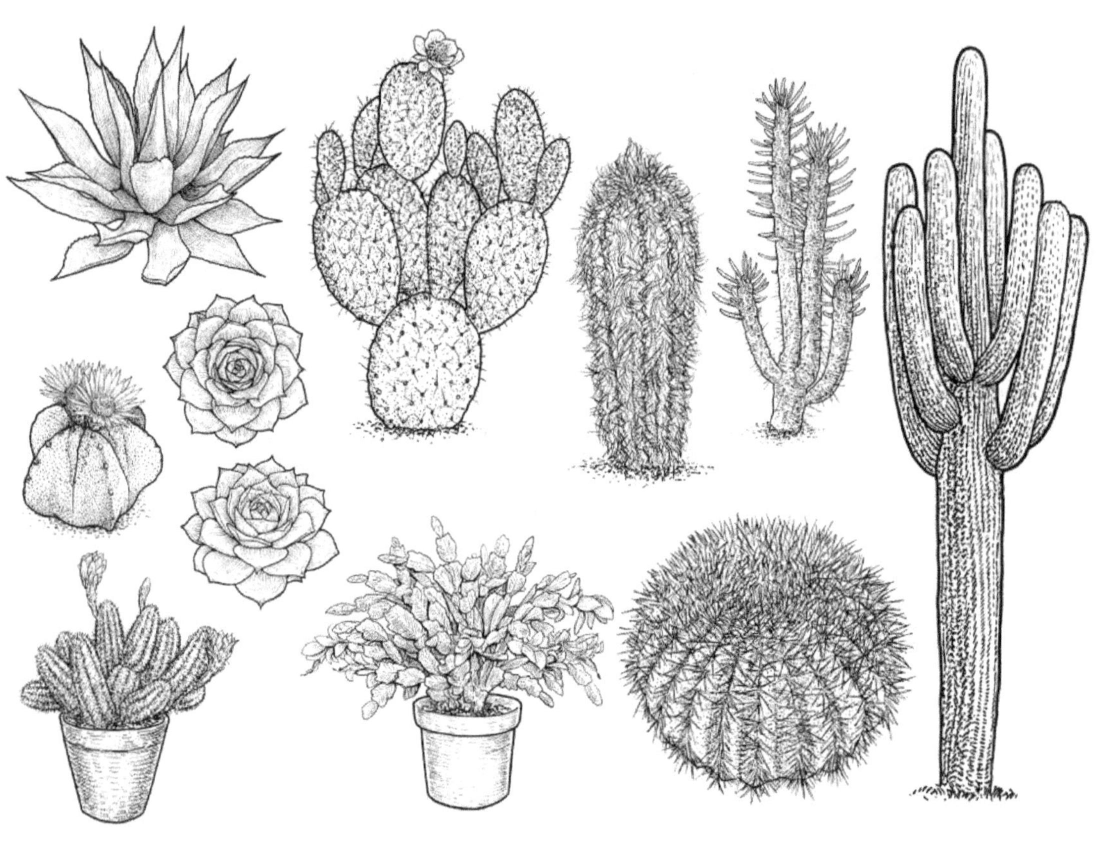

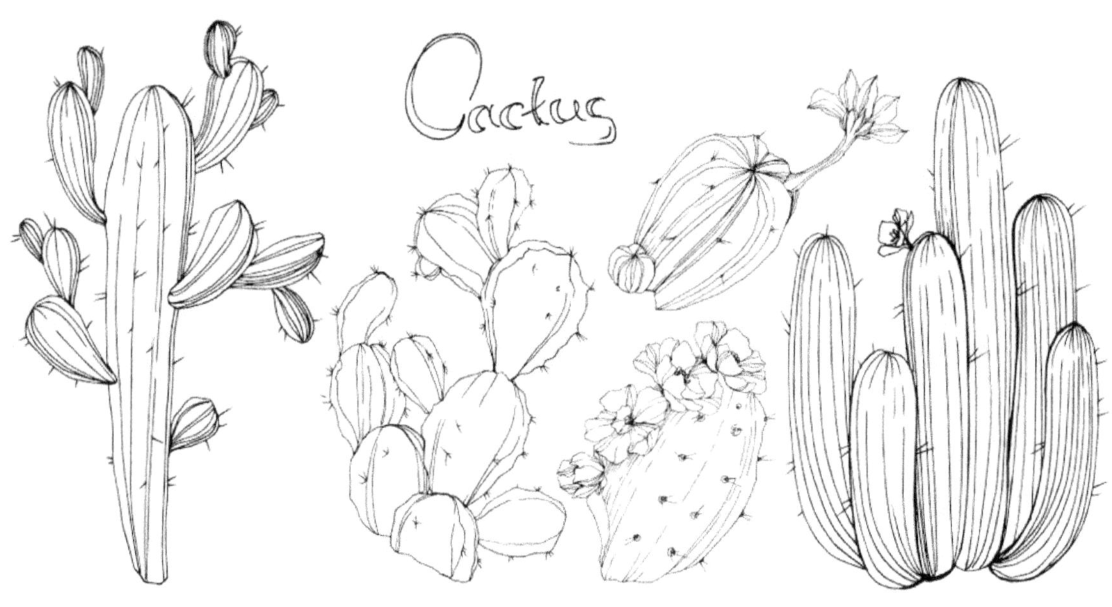
Cactus

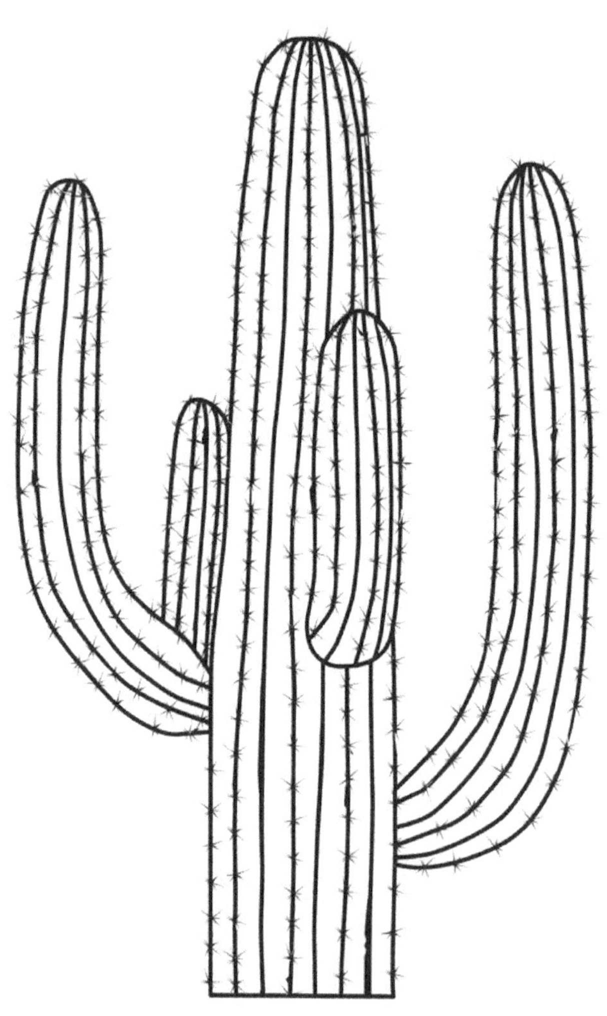

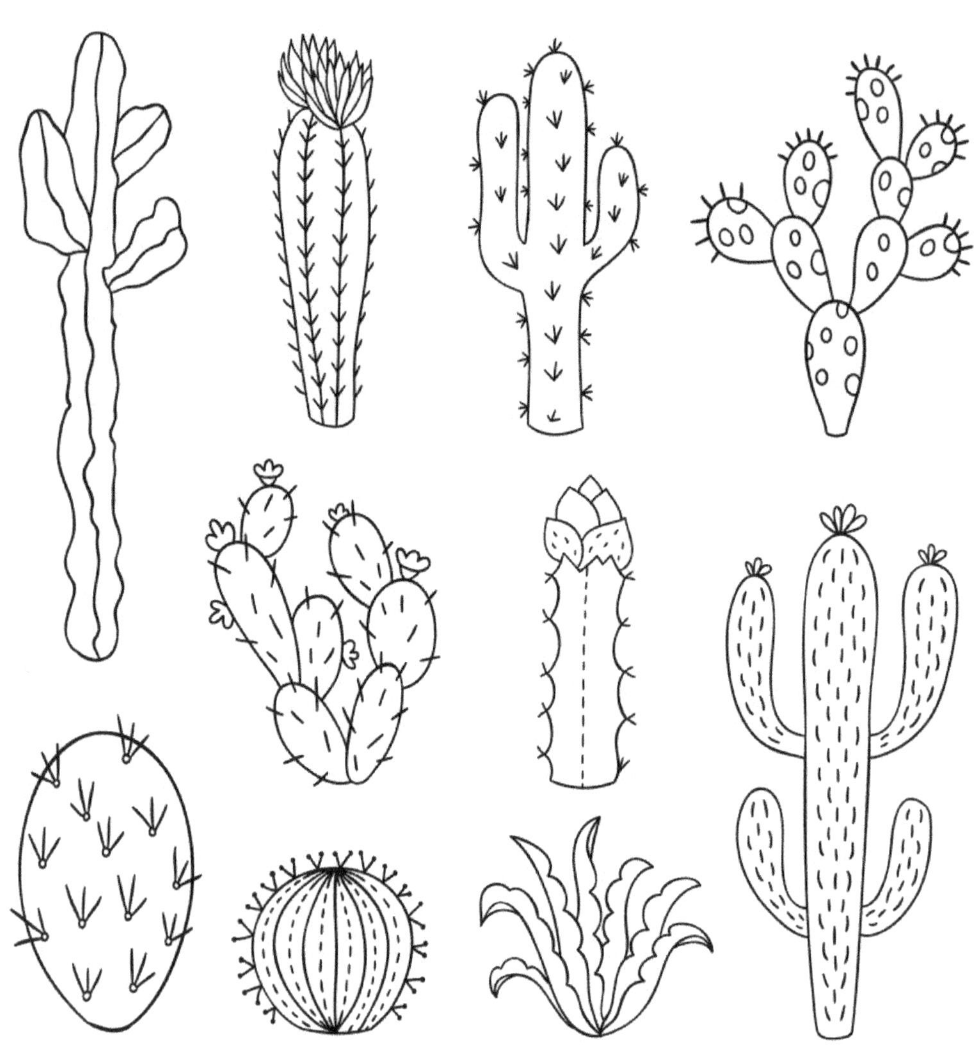

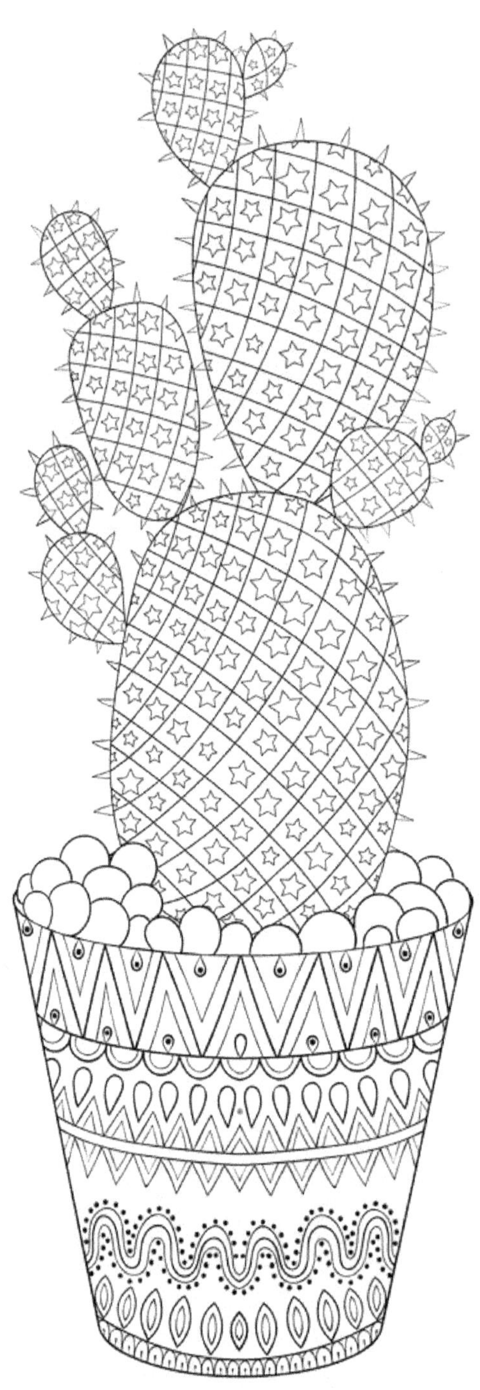

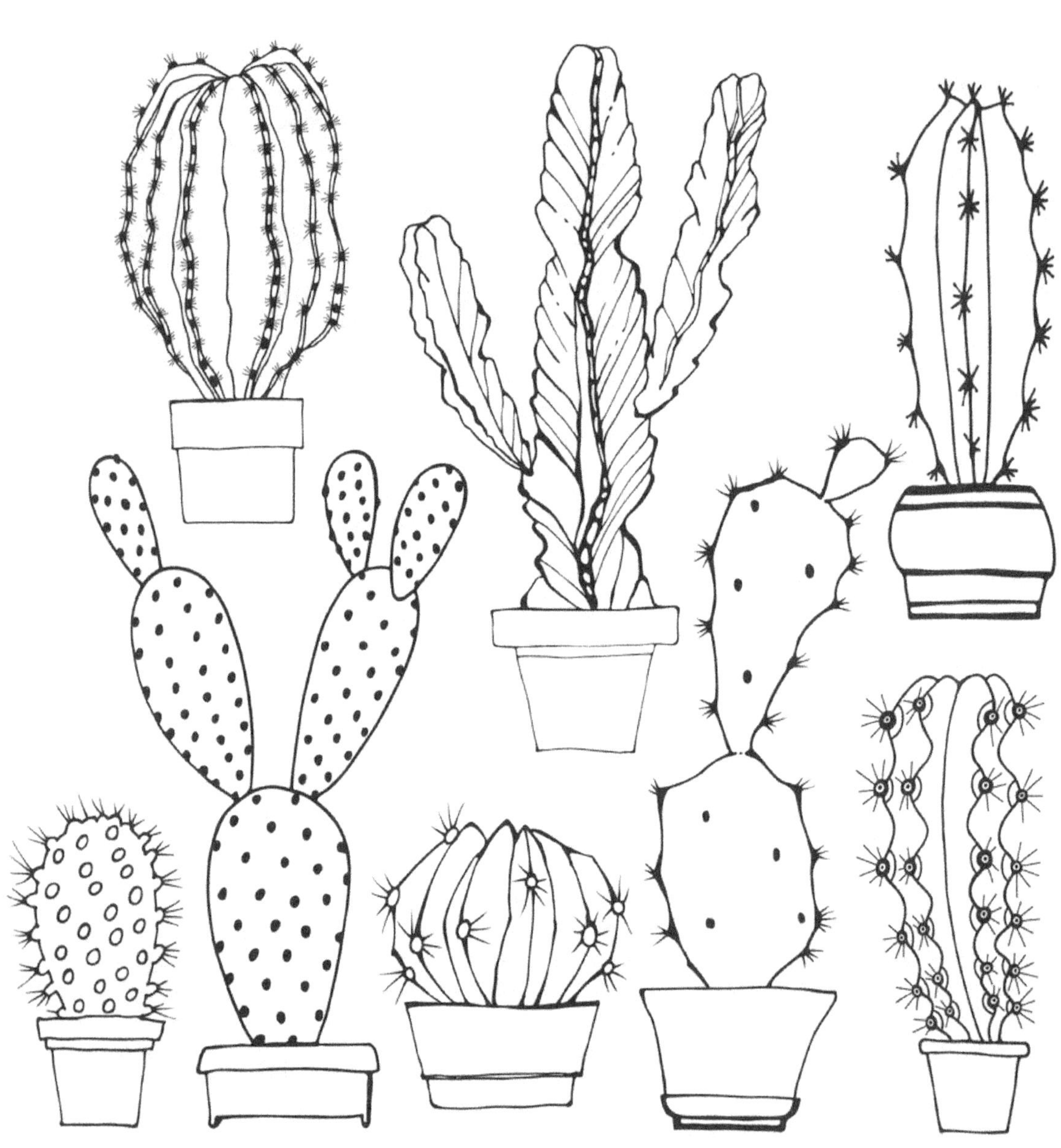